Best Wishes,

Jim Lee

Praise for Fifteen Feet For Free

"*Fifteen Feet For Free* is a great read for anyone who wants to improve their "game" off the court as well as on the court. The inspirational story of Jim's dad, Snook, is worth the price of admission before you even read a word about the foul shot. Jim's view on the importance of setting goals, working hard, maintaining focus, paying attention to detail and having a positive attitude can help anyone at any age. These are the same attributes that we value at Noco Energy and look for in all of our team members."

Jack Catanzaro
- General Manager, Noco Energy Corp.

"Jim Lee's book is a must read for players and coaches at all levels. His simple mechanical and mental approach to free throw shooting is a proven winner. With one instructional visit to our practice before a game we went from a 64% free throw shooting team to 78%. And we won the game. Jim has helped our team almost every year for the past decade."

Pat Donnelly
- Head Basketball Coach at Bishop Ludden HS, Syracuse, NY
  (1987-Present, 432 Wins and Counting)
- New York State Public High School Athletic Association (NYSPHSAA)
  State Champion 1994
- NYSPHSAA Final Four 2001
- 8 New York State Section III Championships
- 12 League Championships

"The beauty of this book is the aggregate impact it will have on players' lives. Jim's father instilled skills in his son to serve him on and off the court for a lifetime. I grew up in Syracuse attending hoop camps and learning from many of the people Jim cites in this book, which enabled me to play Division III college hoops. While I never became a great free throw shooter, the skills in *Fifteen Feet For Free* have served me well in both my personal and professional life."

Tim Giarrusso
- *Chief Operating Officer, Association for the Blind and Visually Impaired-Goodwill, Inc. (2008-Present)*
- *Adjunct Professor, Rochester Institute of Technology (1999-Present)*
- *Player, Rochester Institute of Technology, Rochester, NY (1977-80)*

"Coaches and players of all levels can benefit from this book. Each group will be impressed by the importance of practice and shooting correctly. A system established by the best shooter I have had the pleasure to know."

Jack Halloran
- *Retired Head Basketball Coach at Whitney Point HS, Whitney Point, NY (41 Years and 630 Wins)*
- *Inducted into the NYS Basketball Hall of Fame*
- *Inducted into the National High School Athletic Coaches Association (NHSACA) Hall of Fame*
- *Inducted into the NYSPHSAA Hall of Fame*

"*Fifteen Feet For Free* will improve anyone's free throw shooting, and guess what – if you play golf, it will improve your putting also. I once made 332 consecutive free throws thanks to Jim Lee's instruction. His insights for establishing a consistent, reliable routine are exactly what PGA, LPGA and Champions Tour players work on regularly."

Jim Roy
- *PGA and Champions Tour Player*

"Whether you are a coach or a player, in grade school or college, Jim Lee's *Fifteen Feet For Free* is a must read. Jim's approach – along with tips from some of the greatest foul shooters ever – is simplistic and easy to understand. This book will help make you a confident, and therefore proficient, player when the pressure is on at the end of the game."

Jim Satalin

- National Director, Coaches vs. Cancer (1995-Present)
- Head Basketball Coach, Duquesne University (1982-89)
- Head Basketball Coach, St. Bonaventure University (1973-82)
- Inducted into the St. Bonaventure University Hall of Fame

FIFTEEN FEET FOR FREE

My childhood home – Kirkwood, New York

FIFTEEN FEET FOR FREE

A simple guide to foul shooting for players at any
level—from the driveway to the NBA

JIM LEE

authorHOUSE®

AuthorHouse™
1663 Liberty Drive
Bloomington, IN 47403
www.authorhouse.com
Phone: 1-800-839-8640

Published by AuthorHouse   04/27/2012

ISBN: 978-1-4685-2987-6 (sc)
ISBN: 978-1-4685-2986-9 (hc)
ISBN: 978-1-4685-2985-2 (e)

Library of Congress Control Number: 2012901342

Any people depicted in stock imagery provided by Thinkstock are models, and such images are being used for illustrative purposes only.
Certain stock imagery © Thinkstock.

This book is printed on acid-free paper.

Because of the dynamic nature of the Internet, any web addresses or links contained in this book may have changed since publication and may no longer be valid. The views expressed in this work are solely those of the author and do not necessarily reflect the views of the publisher, and the publisher hereby disclaims any responsibility for them.

This book is dedicated in memory of my dad, Harold "Snook" Lee, and to all disabled veterans (past, present, and future) who have fought for our country's freedom and way of life.

CONTENTS

Foreword.. 1

Introduction 3

1   Purpose 7

2   Mechanics 11

3   Practice 29

4   Mindset 33

5   Goals 35

6   Philosophies 37

7   Benchmark... 67

Afterword.. 81

Epilogue.. 85

Notes 87

Acknowledgements 89

About the Author... 91

FOREWORD

It was 40 years ago when I first met Jimmy Lee. We were freshmen at Syracuse University and were at our first meeting for the basketball team at Manley Field House. There was a little nervousness in the air as we were finally going to meet our teammates for that year, and hopefully the years to follow. My roommate, Rudy Hackett, and I had known each other in high school as we played against each other in the final game of our high school season. Rudy was the starting center for an undefeated Mount Vernon squad which had Mike Young (Manhattan College) at forward, and in the backcourt had future professionals Earl Tatum (Marquette University, drafted by the Lakers) and Gus Williams (University of Southern California, NBA All Star with Seattle Supersonics). At this meeting, Coach Roy Danforth introduced the varsity players which included Dennis "Sweet D" DuVal, Greg "Kid" Kohls, Mark Wadach, Bobby Dooms and Jimmy's older brother Mike Lee. Then he introduced the freshmen squad which included a couple of forwards from Indiana, Lou Cotton and Donny Degner, Rudy and myself, and off in the corner our only scholarship guard named Jimmy Lee. He was from a town we never heard of, Kirkwood, New York. Jimmy was a small 6'1", and weighed 150 pounds soaking wet. He had a pageboy haircut, looked about 14 years old and I swore he didn't shave. Rudy and I just looked at each other and thought we were going to be in for a very long freshman season.

So much for first impressions. We quickly discovered that "Young James" Lee would be a tough competitor and the guard you most wanted to run your team. He was unselfish, team oriented and disciplined. Jim never took a bad shot or missed an open pass. Our freshman squad, the Tangerines, posted a 17-1 record losing only at Canisius. But the reason for our success was in large part because of the Kid from Kirkwood. Jimmy was a great shooter, but equally important was his grit and determination. Simply put, Jimmy just hated to lose.

Jimmy showed that same competitiveness on varsity the next year. If Jimmy didn't invent the ability to pick up the offensive charge call, he certainly brought it to a new level. He drew a charge against North Carolina's Phil Ford in the 1975 game that gave us the ball back with seconds left, and set up Jimmy's game winner at the buzzer which propelled us to the school's first Final Four appearance. Taking offensive fouls isn't glamorous and is punishing on your body, but this is one of the many ways Jimmy would do whatever it took to win ballgames.

When it came to foul shooting, there was nobody you would rather have at the line. And Jimmy became "automatic" through hard work and determination. Like picking up offensive fouls, making foul shots doesn't make the top 10 on SportsCenter, but it wins ball games. The art of foul shooting is often overlooked by many coaches and players. Like practicing putting, it probably seems too boring. But as Jimmy points out, many games are won or lost at the foul line. Jimmy would spend hours, before and after practice, working on his shot.

In this book, Jimmy breaks down the mechanics of the foul shot and provides insight into the mental aspects of the free throw. More importantly, he provides excellent instruction for how to maximize your abilities and contributions to your team. Finally, this book is a great tribute to Jimmy's father, Harold Lee, who was an inspiration to Jimmy, his family and all who had the pleasure of knowing him.

Steve Shaw, Esq.
Syracuse University (1971-75)

INTRODUCTION

On September 11, 1924, my father, Harold Francis (Snook) Lee was born in Utica, New York. In 1943 at the age of eighteen, Snook – better known to me as Dad – left Binghamton North High School to enroll in the United States Coast Guard.

On a foggy night in January 1945, while patrolling the East Coast near Martha's Vineyard, a U.S. Destroyer mistakenly crashed into my Dad's ship. Unfortunately, the Destroyer broadsided his ship at the exact point where he was sleeping.

The accident immediately ripped one of his legs off and completely crushed the other, which was left barely attached to his body. Years later, my father recounted that, as he was floating in the water trying to stay conscious, he could see most of his bunkmates scrambling for safety – leaving him behind for dead.

To this day, my brothers, sister, and I still acknowledge Moses Duncan for our existence. Mr. Duncan was one of the ship's cooks, and it was Mr. Duncan who saved my dad's life. He slung my father over his shoulder, bringing him to safety, and getting him the necessary help. If not for Moses, my father would have probably bled to death on that fateful January night in the ice-cold Atlantic water.

Snook – complete with high doses of morphine and tourniquets on his legs – was transported to a Navy hospital in Newport, Rhode Island, accompanied by one of the ship's doctors. From Rhode Island, he was transferred to the Naval Hospital in Philadelphia, Pennsylvania. He spent approximately three years there, where he underwent a series of operations, rehabilitated his legs, received artificial limbs, and learned to walk all over again.

For the rest of his life, my father used artificial legs and a wheelchair to get around – neither of which stopped him from living a normal life. In 1950, he married my mother, Constance Janet Browne and together they had six children: Mike, myself, Patricia, Tim, Bob, and Dave. My parents were also blessed with 17 grandchildren. My dad

3

never let his wheelchair get in the way; instead he improvised by taking his grandchildren for rides on it up and down the hardwood floors at his home.

*　　*　　*

Snook loved watching sports of any kind. He was a Ted Williams and Boston Red Sox fan, and in his eyes Sam Huff and the New York Giants could do no wrong. Before his accident, he was an avid basketball player at Binghamton North High School. My dad's love of and involvement in sports was passed on to my siblings and I at a young age.

Growing up, my dad would pitch to the entire neighborhood as we played baseball in the yard. He would wheel himself to the pitcher's mound, rarely asking for any help getting there. During football season, we would throw the football around in the driveway. Dad also had a 30-foot by 30-foot blacktop court installed in the backyard so that we could play basketball all year-round. From his chair, he would shoot baskets with us; and when he wasn't shooting, he would hang out and just watch us play. He rarely missed any of our baseball, football or basketball games. Following a game, we were typically met with, "good game" or "tough one tonight" – simple words, yet we knew what he meant.

My older brother, Mike, and I were both fortunate enough to play collegiate basketball at Syracuse University. Mike got to Syracuse first, in 1969. As a kid, I always loved playing alongside Mike; thus, when Coach Roy Danforth and Syracuse offered me a scholarship, I gladly accepted and joined my older brother, playing at Syracuse from 1971 to 1975. To this day, I am forever grateful to Coach Danforth, Coach Jim Boeheim, and Coach Bill Vesp for giving me an opportunity to get an education and to compete on the court.

My mother and father came to nearly every home game, sitting in the two seats at the end of the first row behind the Syracuse bench in Manley Field House, Syracuse's home before the Carrier Dome. Both Mike and I knew that Dad got great enjoyment and satisfaction watching us play. Being able to perform and play as hard as I could was of the utmost importance to me. One of the reasons I loved playing basketball so much was because my father was unable to walk. Simply watching him go about his daily routine, I could not help but learn how to compete and how to prevail.

My father took his last breath on April 16, 2003, at the age of 78. His death certificate cites "vascular disease" as the cause of death. Doctors said he should have passed away 16 years earlier, at the age of 62, according to statistics regarding double amputees.

Snook touched the lives of each and every person with whom he came in contact with. He had that "never give up" attitude and he truly lived every day as if it was his last. I remember him telling us, "I should have been gone a long time ago, so every day is a bonus for me." I believe that this positive attitude contributed to the extended length of time he was able to live his life.

*   *   *

Since 2004, my friends and I have been running a golf tournament in my father's honor. Out of respect for Dad and all that he represented, 100% of the proceeds from this tournament are donated to help veterans injured in our country's wars and battles. [See the Epilogue for more information.]

Fifty percent of the proceeds from the sale of this book will be donated to the *Entrepreneurship Bootcamp for Veterans* with Disabilities (EBV) at Syracuse University's Martin J. Whitman School of Management. The EBV began at Syracuse University in 2007; there are currently seven other universities nationwide that offer this program, all working in conjunction with one another. They are the University of Connecticut, Cornell University, Florida State University, Louisiana State University, Purdue University, Texas A&M University, and UCLA. This program is free to the veterans that are accepted to participate; more information can be found at http://whitman.syr.edu/ebv/.

In writing this book, I hope to help many basketball players with their foul shooting, both male and female, across all skill levels – middle school, high school, college, and even the NBA.

In some small way, this book acts as a "thank you," to the many veterans whose lives have been impacted while fighting for our country and our freedom. Now, let's play ball.

My dad aboard his ship, 1944

My parents on my wedding day, 1983

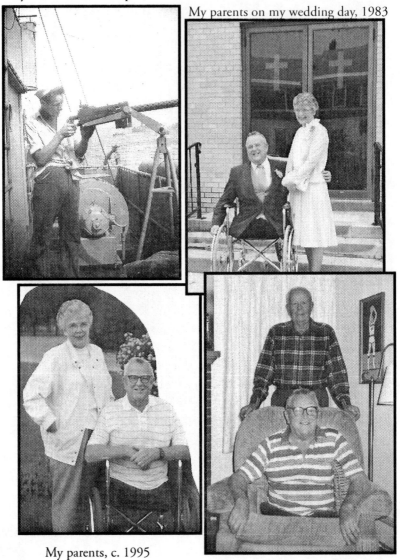

My parents, c. 1995

My dad and Uncle Maury(retired,
Colonel US Air Force), c. 1998

1

PURPOSE

At times, foul shooting seems to be the forgotten part of basketball; however, I would argue that the foul shot is one of the most important aspects of the game. How many times do you see a team lose a game by one or two points because of missed free throws?

I am not the best free throw shooter in the world, nor do I profess to be. However, over the years I have helped a number of individuals of all ages become better free throw shooters. When speaking to a high school team at the outset of a season, or spending one-on-one time with someone in my driveway, I cannot stress enough how important it is to capitalize on the opportunity presented at the "charity stripe."

I played basketball for Syracuse University from 1971 to 1975, and was the team's co-captain my senior year. Following my college career, in 1975, I signed a contract with the San Antonio Spurs of the ABA. Additionally, I was drafted by the Cleveland Cavaliers in the fifth round of the NBA draft. I would have loved to have made it at the next level, fulfilling my dream; but with a 6'2", 160-pound frame, I knew the odds were against me. To top it off, I wasn't the quickest guy in the world. Realistically, I knew my chances of making the ABA or NBA were slim. I gave it my best shot, but unfortunately didn't play as well as I knew I was capable of playing while in San Antonio.

Every basketball player has his or her calling card; for me, I had a better-than-average jump shot. Of course, there is a reason for that: I spent hours upon hours practicing and shooting jump shots when I was growing up. I particularly excelled at the free throw line, taking advantage of the "free" points offered during the course of a game. In my sophomore season at Syracuse, 1972-73, I ranked fifth nationally in free throw shooting. During that year's NCAA tournament, I was tied for first in the nation, but I missed one foul shot against Furman in the sub-regional game that resulted in my descent to fifth. That season, my free throw percentage of 88.6% put me in Syracuse's history books with the highest single season free throw shooting percentage. My senior year, I finished sixth in the country at 86.0%. Records are made to be broken, though. After his 2002-03 season and Syracuse's first National Championship ever, Gerry McNamara broke my 30-year record with a free throw shooting percentage of 90.9%.

During my final year at Syracuse, 1974-75, we were fortunate enough to play in the school's first ever Final Four in San Diego, California, along with UCLA (coached by John Wooden), Kentucky (Joe B. Hall), and Louisville (Denny Crum). UCLA won the 1975 Final Four, sending Coach Wooden into retirement with another NCAA Championship. Our road to the Final Four included victories against LaSalle in the sub-regional game, North Carolina and finally Kansas State in the Eastern Regional Championship. One of the highlights of my basketball career came in our game against North Carolina. With Syracuse trailing by 1 point with 27 seconds remaining, we worked the ball around and held the ball for 1 last shot. With 3 seconds left, I made an 18-foot jump shot from the left side of the foul line to upset the Tar Heels, making it one of the biggest victories in Syracuse basketball history (at least, in my opinion).

At the close of the tournament, I was selected by the NCAA Tournament Committee as a member of the Final Four's All-Tournament Team, along with Kevin Grevey of Kentucky, Allen Murphy of Louisville, and David Myers and Richard Washington of UCLA. Additionally, I was named leading scorer of the entire NCAA tournament. I was also selected to the NCAA Eastern Regional All-Tournament Team and the ECAC All East All Star Team. At season's end, I was honored as a Helms Foundation All-American and awarded the Lew Andreas Award for Most Valuable Player at Syracuse. Subsequently, in 1984, I received Syracuse University's Vic Hanson Medal of Excellence Award; in 2000, I was selected to Syracuse University's All Century Basketball team; and in 2009, I was named a Syracuse University Letter Winner of Distinction, which is the highest honor awarded by the Syracuse Athletic Department to a former student-athlete letter winner.

Although we were not crowned National Champions in 1975, the recognition I received for my performance in the tournament is something that will be forever printed in the NCAA record books as tangible feats that I will always look back on with pride.

As many of you will find out as life goes on, and as I learned as the sun set on my short-lived one-week professional athletic career, you don't always get what you want. To quote one of my father's favorite sayings, "Be thankful for what you've got." Live your life with gratitude and respect for others, and do not regret one day while living your life, because you never know when it might change forever. [See Figure 1.1][1]

Jim Lee
6'2", 160 lbs
Windsor HS (Windsor, NY)
Syracuse University

Year	Class	G	FG	FGA	FG%	FT	FTA	FT%	3P	3PA	3P%	PTS	PPG	ASST	APG	REB	RPG
at Syracuse University (Freshman Team)																	
1971-72	Fr	18	135	262	58.2	69	82	84.2	N/A	N/A	N/A	339	18.8	88	4.8	87	4.8
at Syracuse University																	
1972-73	So	29	83	187	44.4	93	105	88.6	N/A	N/A	N/A	259	8.9	47	1.6	49	1.7
1973-74	Jr	26	152	304	50.0	52	64	81.3	N/A	N/A	N/A	356	13.7	107	4.1	84	3.2
1974-75	Sr	32	226	464	48.7	98	114	86.0	N/A	N/A	N/A	550	17.2	115	3.6	99	2.7
Total		87	461	955	48.3	243	283	85.9	N/A	N/A	N/A	1,165	13.4	269	3.1	262	2.7
at Windsor HS																	
1967-68	Fr	19	70	209	33.4	41	59	69.5	N/A	N/A	N/A	181	9.5	N/A	N/A	65	3.4
1968-69	So	21	116	271	42.8	77	93	82.8	N/A	N/A	N/A	309	14.7	N/A	N/A	117	5.6
1969-70	Jr	20	177	358	49.4	170	196	86.7	N/A	N/A	N/A	524	26.2	N/A	N/A	213	10.7
1970-71	Sr	21	212	363	58.1	162	179	90.5	N/A	N/A	N/A	586	27.9	N/A	N/A	249	11.8
Total		81	575	1,201	47.9	450	527	85.4	N/A	N/A	N/A	1,600	19.8	N/A	N/A	644	7.9

Figure 1.1

2

MECHANICS

Shooting a free throw is not as difficult as some players portray. It can be accomplished through a simple process or routine, and a lot of practice, all done in a serious manner.

It is much easier to shoot a foul shot when you are by yourself than it is in front of a packed arena with the game on the line, regardless of the level of competition you are playing against. For this reason, it is important to have a repetitive process that you can fall back on in game situations, allowing your reflex action to take over. This can only be accomplished with proper practice and repetition.

The process outlined below should be followed each time you approach the foul line. The total process should become second nature the more you work at it.

The Process: 1. Balance
2. Concentration (Eyes on the Target)
3. Elbow In and the Basketball
4. Follow Through

For the average basketball player, foul shooting can be an avenue to get on the floor and get more playing time. The best foul shooters are typically on the court at the end of a game, as long as they are not a detriment to the team in other parts of the game.

BALANCE

Stepping to the foul line, you must be on balance. This does not only apply to free throws, but to any type of jump shot. A foul shot or a jump shot should never be taken if you are not on balance.

Feet Position: The first element is positioning. You should position your feet in a stance that makes you feel comfortable. This will be different for each individual, as what is comfortable for one person may not be comfortable for another. A rule of thumb: your feet will probably be in a position as if you were standing and talking to your friends. This is generally a "comfortable" position.

When I am at the foul line, I find it most effective when my feet are approximately shoulder width apart – my right foot slightly in front of my left foot because I am right-handed. The opposite is true for a left-hand shooter, for whom the left foot should be slightly in front of the right. [See Figure 2.1]

Figure 2.1 Feet approximately shoulder width apart

Relax and Take Two Dribbles: Once your body is balanced with your feet in the proper position, take two dribbles with the ball bouncing in front of your right foot. This is part of the process and will help keep you mentally balanced as well as physically balanced.

Perhaps certain players want to appear "cool" at the free throw line. I see many players attempting different things at the foul line – for example: flipping the ball in their hands; putting the ball around their back; bouncing the ball five or six times; and swaying back and forth while bouncing the ball. This extra movement does not help with balance.

Upon approaching the foul line, there is only one objective – make the shot.

Ball Position: The best place to position your hands on the basketball are on its seams, so you can read the writing. Therefore, when you end up shooting, it becomes very easy to see if the ball has the proper rotation. [See Figure 2.2]

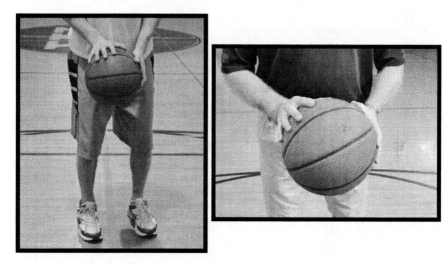

Figure 2.2 Read the writing on the ball and place your hands accordingly.

Body Set Up: Your shoulders should be square to the basket, with your eyes on the target. Notice that age or gender does not affect this positioning. [See Figure 2.3]

Figure 2.3 Shoulders square to the basket

It is important to minimize any excess movement at the foul line. **The less movement . . . the less room for error.**

Game Plan

Once you have established balance, with your feet shoulder width apart, take two dribbles. Next, position your hands properly on the ball and square your shoulders to the basket . . .

CONCENTRATION (EYES ON THE TARGET)

Once on balance, immediately turn your focus to the rim. This is your target. You should have total concentration on the basket, with your eyes on the target until the basketball goes through the net.

There are a variety of opinions as to **where** on the rim one should focus. It doesn't matter which part of the rim that you look at – the front, just over the front, the back, the whole rim, etc. Whatever your target may be, **make sure you look at this same spot every single time you are at the foul line.** [See Figure 2.4]

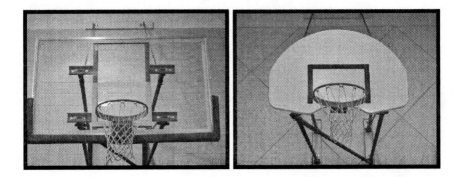

Figure 2.4 The Target – Keep your eyes on the basket

At the foul line, I always looked at the whole rim and visualized the ball going in the center of the rim each and every time. Keep your eyes on the target until the ball goes through the basket. **Do not follow the ball with your eyes.** Once the basketball leaves your hand, there is nothing that you can do that will change the flight of the ball; therefore, there is no need to take your eyes off the target.

Too many players lift their head after the ball is released in order to follow the flight of the ball. A movement as small as this, takes the body out of balance, if only for a moment. By following the ball with your eyes, your head will lift up and your shoulders will move back just enough so that your body is not in complete balance.

I am confident that your free throw percentage will improve by keeping your eyes on the target until the ball goes through the hoop.

Keep your eyes on the target! Concentrate! Do not move your head!
[See Figure 2.5]

Figure 2.5 Eyes on the target

It is important to minimize any excess movement at the foul line.
The less movement . . . the less room for error.

Game Plan

Once you have established balance with your feet shoulder width apart, take two dribbles. Next, position your hands properly on the basketball and square your shoulders to the basket, *with your eyes focused, concentrating only on the target . . .*

ELBOW IN AND THE BASKETBALL

The next step in the foul shooting process is to keep your elbow in when shooting the ball. Like balance, this action is also different for each player. You must have your elbow in as you start to raise your arm to shoot the basketball. This will help the ball to move in a straight line toward the basket.

The ball should not rest on the palm of your hand. Be sure you are controlling the basketball with your fingertips. Keeping the ball on your fingertips will allow you to have better control of the basketball. The more control you have of the ball, the more likely it is to go through the basket. [See Figure 2.6]

Figure 2.6 Palms off the ball with fingertip control

Your left hand should be placed slightly on the left side of the ball, acting only as a guide. For a right-hand shooter, the only purpose the left hand serves is to keep the ball from falling out of the shooting hand. The opposite is true for a left-hand shooter, for whom the right hand acts as the guide. [See Figure 2.7]

Figure 2.7 The guide hand is the left hand for a right-hand shooter

Picture yourself throwing darts at a dartboard. This is the same action your arm takes when shooting a foul shot. Straighten your arm toward the target, whether the target is the dartboard or the basket.

Once the ball is in good position in your hands as previously discussed, the only thing you have to do is straighten your arm. Shooting a foul shot (or a jump shot) is that simple – bend your knees, keep your eyes on the basket, and just straighten out your arm.

Each player's motions will differ due to his or her own physical make-up. Try to have your elbow in as much as possible. Notice that age or gender does not play a part in the set up with your elbow and the basketball. [See Figure 2.8]

Figure 2.8 Elbow in as much as possible

Figure 2.9 is of me at the foul line in 1975 and in 2011. In both photos, the ball is about ready to leave my hands, yet my eyes remain on the target and my elbow is in. The ball is resting just off the palm of my shooting hand, my fingertips are in control, and my guide hand is helping to stabilize the ball. My eyes do not leave the basket until the ball goes through the rim.

Figure 2.9 1975 and 2011; Notice my eyes are fixated on the basket

It is important to minimize any excess movement at the foul line.
The less movement . . . the less room for error.

Once you have established balance with your feet shoulder width apart, take two dribbles. Next, position your hands properly on the basketball and square your shoulders to the basket, with your eyes focused, concentrating only on the target. *The ball should rest just off the palm of your hand, on your fingertips with your elbow in as much as possible . . .*

FOLLOW THROUGH

The final step in the process is the follow through. At this point, BEND YOUR KNEES, extend your arm straight to the rim as the ball leaves your shooting hand, and follow through; your index finger should cut the rim in half when following through. So long as the index finger is the last part of your hand that touches the ball before it is released, the ball should go straight and into the basket.

This motion should automatically keep your wrist straight as you extend your arm toward the rim. Keep your eyes on the target and your head still. Notice that age or gender does not make the follow through any different. [See Figures 2.10 and 2.11]

Figure 2.10 Follow through with your eyes on target.

Figure 2.11 Your eyes should not leave the target

Notice how my arm is extended upward as I follow through in Figure 2.11. I always extended my arm upward instead of outward in order to get more arc on my shot. The extra arc makes the basket a little bit bigger, as the ball is coming in at a steeper angle to the rim.

Figures 2.12 and 2.13 show the follow through from a different angle – behind the shooter. Notice that my hand follows through to the middle of the rim as the ball goes through the net. There is neither head nor shoulder movement.

Figure 2.12

Figure 2.13

Figure 2.12 Follow through to the middle of the rim with index finger

Figure 2.13 Head and shoulders remain still as the ball goes through net

It is important to minimize any excess movement at the foul line.
The less movement . . . the less room for error.

Game Plan

Once you have established balance with your feet shoulder width apart, take two dribbles. Next, position your hands properly on the basketball and square your shoulders to the basket, with your eyes focused, concentrating only on the target. The ball should rest just off the palm of your hand, on your fingertips with your elbow in as much as possible. *Bend your knees and follow through, keeping your head still and your eyes on the basket until the ball goes through the net.*

After taking thousands and thousands of foul shots, I had this repetitive process clearly engrained in my mind. The only thing I needed to do as I approached the foul line was to **BEND MY KNEES AND FOLLOW THROUGH**. I blocked out everything and just focused on myself and the basket. The rest of the process became automatic.

The art of shooting free throws is simple – do not try to make it any harder. And the more you practice, the simpler it gets. Furthermore, confidence breeds success. The more confident you are at the foul line, the better your foul shooting percentage should be.
[See Figures 2.14 and 2.15]

Figure 2.14   **Figure 2.15**

Figure 2.14 Balance, shoulders square, and eyes on target

Figure 2.15 Elbow in, bend your knees, and follow through

3

PRACTICE

Practice: *"to perform or work at repeatedly so as to become proficient"*[1]

As in any sport (or, for that matter, anything else you do in life), the more you practice, the better you get. Let me restate that . . . The more you properly practice, the better you get.

Growing up in Kirkwood, New York, I got in the habit of shooting at least 100 foul shots per day from elementary school through college. Every day, I would religiously shoot my foul shots and record the results. I wanted to be the best foul shooter to ever play the game.

The day before each game at Windsor High School in Windsor, New York, our basketball coach, Jack Collins, would buy a soda for the player that made the most shots out of 25 attempts. I made it one of my goals to win that soft drink every single time. That was 40 years ago and, to this day, I can still vividly remember my desire to win. My senior year in high school, my free throw percentage was 90.5%.

As a college basketball player, we would shoot at least 25 free throws as a team on a daily basis. To this day, I can still vividly remember my desire to have the highest percentage each day from the 15-foot line.

To become a good free throw shooter, or to become a better free throw shooter, you must practice. Every day, practice the proper way. Each day, write down how many shots you make out of 100 attempts, and try to do better the next day. Use the enclosed spreadsheets to track your progress. [See Chapter 7: *Benchmark*]

I used to practice regardless of the weather, be it rain or snow. Unfortunately when it snowed, I had to first shovel the court before I could shoot. If it got too cold out, I'd put on a pair of winter gloves and shoot. Battling the elements of upstate New York helped me to concentrate and also gave me confidence no matter what the environment.

The most free throws I ever made in a row were 423. I still remember the one shot that I missed. The ball hit the front of the rim, then the back, then the front and fell off.

You might think this repetitive shooting is boring, but it becomes somewhat of a game, where you are ultimately competing against yourself. The feeling you get when you make your first 100 out of 100 is incredible.

It is a simple fact – if you don't practice, you will not become a better free throw shooter.

For me, the practice paid off. In terms of free throw percentage, I was the fifth best Division 1 free throw shooter in the country in 1972-73 and the sixth best in 1974-75. Throughout my college career, I am confident that I received more playing time due to my success at the "charity stripe."

OVERTIME DRILLS

1. Not only would I shoot 100 foul shots a day, I would shoot free throws to emulate game situations. Shoot two foul shots or shoot one and one; go through different drills from running, dribbling, and shooting; go back to the foul line for one or two more free throws; do more drills; and go back to the foul line for more game-situation free throws.

2. Find a friend; have shooting competition games. My brother, Mike, and I would have foul shooting contests all the time against each other.

3. Practice your form in front of a mirror. I used to look into a mirror and check my form regularly. It is a great way to make sure you are on balance, your hands are properly positioned on the ball, and very easy to check your elbow and follow through.

4. Lie on your back and practice finger tip control with your palms off the ball, elbow in and follow through. Toss the ball up to the ceiling and see how close to the ceiling you can get without hitting the ceiling.

5. Sit in a chair and repeat drill 4 (from above). Practice your form – fingertip control with your palms off the ball, elbow in and follow through to improve the feel of the ball in your hands.
6. Practice enough so the basketball feels like an extension of your arms and hands. You will become more confident the more comfortable you are with the ball.
7. Practice without the basketball. Visualize your routine, or process, and see the ball all the way through the basket.

SNOOK NOTES

There is no substitute for hard work and practice. It can take you to another level. Learn to practice the right way as you work to improve your foul shooting. You'd be surprised how the proper work ethic you use practicing will help you later on in the game of life.

Picture yourself in my father's position. The time and effort he put forth in practice was intended for one thing. He made up his mind that he was going to learn to walk again, no matter how much time it took. Practice and hard work paid off for him as he learned to walk again; you are practicing to become a better foul shooter. The same principle applies to both, only for different reasons.

PRACTICE! PRACTICE! PRACTICE!

4

MINDSET

The mental approach to shooting a free throw is just as important as the shot itself, if not more important. As soon as you are fouled and approach the foul line, your attitude should be, "I am going to make this shot." Never go to the foul line thinking anything else.

Whenever I stepped to the foul line, I immediately pictured myself in my backyard in Kirkwood, New York, where I had previously taken and made countless foul shots. The backyard was my comfort zone. You, too, should have a foul line comfort zone – a place that makes your 15-foot range invincible.

I firmly believed I would make every shot I took at the foul line. Not that I made every shot, but that was how I thought. Stepping to the line with a positive attitude enhanced my free throw percentage. If you think you are going to make it, the odds of making it are better than if you don't think you are going to make it.

Foul shots are unique in the world of athletics; they are the only "free" opportunities without any defense present. That is why they call them free throws. For example, football, baseball, hockey, soccer, and tennis have no free offensive opportunities without the presence of a defense.

Once again, if you can improve your free throw shooting and become a good (or even great) foul shooter, you may get more playing time. The better foul shooters are normally on the court at the end of the game, when each and every possession is crucial.

OVERTIME DRILLS

1. Prepare yourself for the pressure moment and look forward to it.
2. Visualize yourself at the foul line with no time on the clock and calmly making two foul shots to win the game. See it happen before it actually happens. You'd be surprised at the result.
3. *Psycho-Cybernetics*, by Maxwell Maltz[1], was recommended to me while in college, and I found it incredibly useful.
    It discusses a man rehearsing his golf shot before actually striking the ball; the same concept is easily transferable to the foul shot.
4. **Block everything out, except for yourself and the basket. Focus and let your repetitive process take control.**
5. Remember, the steps to shooting a foul shot are always the same, regardless of how many seconds are left on the clock or the score of the game.

SNOOK NOTES

My dad's mental attitude was unbelievable. I never once heard him complain about losing his legs. The word "disabled" was not a part of his vocabulary.

I can remember my future father-in-law saying to me just before I got married, "Jim, I have never met a happier person in my life than your dad. He always has a smile on his face." My father had two choices after he was injured: 1) feel sorry for himself and live the rest of his life in self pity; or 2) make the best of the situation that was given to him. He obviously drifted toward the positive and chose to be thankful for what he had; he was strong enough mentally to maintain that mindset the rest of his life.

My dad used this mindset to get on with his life; your mindset at the foul line is to be positive, block out everything except yourself and the basket, and visualize the ball going through the hoop each and every time.

FOCUS! POSITIVE ATTITUDE!

5

GOALS

At the free throw line, the goal is simple: make each and every shot taken. Your target goal should always be 100%. If this is not your goal when you step to the line, odds are you will never be the best foul shooter you can be. Change your mindset and strive to be *your* best.

My career foul shooting percentage at Syracuse University was 85.9% – leaving 14.1% room for improvement.

OVERTIME DRILLS

1. Set a goal for yourself to improve your free throw percentage each year you are a part of an organized team.
2. Set a goal for yourself, shoot 100 foul shots a day and record them. Benchmark yourself. Be better today than you were yesterday.
3. When you are practicing, never leave the court unless you make your last foul shot attempted. Always leave on a made basket. It does wonders for your mind.
4. Understand why you miss a foul shot. It's okay to miss, as long as you know *why* you missed. You can always make an adjustment to improve your chances for the next shot.
5. Set a realistic goal – be as good as you can possibly be.

SNOOK NOTES

My dad's goal was simple: learn to walk again. Not only did he learn to walk again, he did anything he made up his mind to do. If you set goals for yourself, you can achieve anything, as long as you put your mind to it and strive to follow through.

When Coach Roy Danforth received the Vic Hanson Medal of Excellence Award from Syracuse University in 1987, he mentioned his former players with one or two word comments. When he came to my name, "Jimmy Lee – all heart" – that was the best compliment I could have received. Every time I picked up a basketball, I played as hard as I possibly could. I learned this by simply watching my father live his life.

The goals in my life are simple and are attributable to my father. If implemented as they relate to the game of basketball, they should make you a better player and a better free throw shooter. Play the game the right way, as there is a difference between right and wrong. Strive to be your best. Practice and work hard. Make up your mind to become a better free throw shooter and improve your game.

PRACTICE! PROPER MINDSET! SET GOALS!

6

PHILOSOPHIES

What is your thought process

as you approach the free throw line?

For additional perspective, I spoke with a number of notable college and NBA players, each of whom has a career free throw percentage of 80% or higher. I have had the pleasure of playing with or against the majority of these players; the others I've encountered through personal relationships.

Junior Bridgeman – University of Louisville (1972-75)
Richie Cornwall – Syracuse University (1965-68)
Kevin Grevey – University of Kentucky (1972-75)
John Havlicek – Ohio State University (1959-62)
Marty Headd – Syracuse University (1977-81)
Jeff Hornacek – Iowa State University (1982-86)
Greg "Kid" Kohls – Syracuse University (1969-72)
Mike Lee – Syracuse University (1970-73)
Gerry McNamara – Syracuse University (2002-06)
Patrick Satalin – Catholic University (2002-06)
Danny Schayes – Syracuse University (1977-81)
Dolph Schayes – New York University (1944-48)
John Stockton – Gonzaga University (1980-84)

Once you are handed the ball at the free throw line in a game situation, you only have 10 seconds to shoot. With only 10 seconds, your foul shooting routine needs to be automatic. During their careers, each of the above players developed their own routines and processes that became second nature to them and made them successful at the free throw line. Their tips and methodologies are applicable to players at all levels.

After all, 15 feet is 15 feet. The distance between the free throw line and the basket is always the same, whether in the driveway, at the collegiate level, or in the NBA.

So, I asked each of the above the following question, *"During your playing days, what was your thought process as you approached the free throw line?"*

JUNIOR BRIDGEMAN

Junior Bridgeman played in the NBA for 10 years with the Milwaukee Bucks and 2 years with the Los Angeles Clippers. I had the pleasure of playing against Junior in the 1975 Final Four while he was at Louisville. Unfortunately, we had to play in the consolation game, which Louisville won in overtime, 96-88. Junior had a great pro career, but what I remember was his performance in that game. Junior had 21 points, 11 rebounds, 9 assists, and was 7-8 from the foul line.

When approaching the foul line, Junior commented, "For me, the main thing was to relax and have the same mindset and feeling I did when shooting and practicing by myself."

As it relates to his practice habits, Junior remarked, "I had the same routine: bend my knees; be on balance and do the same thing the same way; block out everything and follow through with the same motion." He developed this routine "through the repetitiveness and practicing of the shot over countless hours."

Junior was a 77.0% free throw shooter in college, but improved to an 84.6% career shooter in the NBA. When asked what he thought was the key for this improvement, he replied, "I believe in college the main focus was not on free throws. In the NBA, it was a job and I developed a different and more serious focus. Why would you miss? Why couldn't you make every one?" Junior's mindset changed. [See Figure 6.1][1]

Ulysses "Junior" Bridgeman

6'5", 210 lbs
Washington HS (East Chicago, IN)
University of Lousville

Year	Class	G	FG	FGA	FG%	FT	FTA	FT%	3P	3PA	3P%	PTS	PPG	ASST	APG	REB	RPG
at the University of Louisville																	
1972-73	So	28	164	338	48.5	58	84	69.0	N/A	N/A	N/A	386	13.8	N/A	N/A	190	6.8
1973-74	Jr	28	179	332	53.9	103	134	76.9	N/A	N/A	N/A	461	16.5	N/A	N/A	237	8.5
1974-75	Sr	31	187	356	52.5	127	156	81.4	N/A	N/A	N/A	501	16.1	N/A	N/A	230	7.4
Total		87	530	1,026	51.7	288	374	77.0	N/A	N/A	N/A	1,348	15.5	N/A	N/A	657	7.6
in the NBA																	
1975-87	N/A	849	4,801	10,099	47.5	1,875	2,216	84.6	40	164	24.4	11,517	13.6	2,066	2.4	2,995	3.5

Figure 6.1

RICHIE CORNWALL

I played against Richie Cornwall in the Eastern League in the 1970's. I knew him by name before then, but that was the first opportunity I had to meet him. Richie graduated from Syracuse in 1968 and was a draft choice of the New York Knicks.

Richie held both the single season and career free throw percentage records when he graduated from Syracuse. I surpassed his single season mark in 1973; in 2006, Gerry McNamara broke Richie's career record, which he had held for 38 years.

When asked about his thoughts as he approached the foul line, he replied, "I had no thought but nailing the shot. It was purely concentration and repetition to make the shot."

Richie had been a Health and Physical Education teacher for 33 years in the Scranton, Pennsylvania area before he retired. He also coached the high school tennis team for 25 years. He remains an avid tennis player, competes regularly and still teaches the game of tennis. [See Figure 6.2][2]

Richie Cornwall
5'11", 160 lbs
Neshaminy HS (Penndel, PA)
Syracuse University

at Syracuse University

Year	Class	G	FG	FGA	FG%	FT	FTA	FT%	3P	3PA	3P%	PTS	PPG	ASST	APG	REB	RPG
1965-66	So	24	60	137	43.8	41	50	82.0	N/A	N/A	N/A	161	6.7	N/A	N/A	45	1.9
1966-67	Jr	26	140	343	40.8	103	117	88.0	N/A	N/A	N/A	383	14.7	N/A	N/A	87	3.3
1967-68	Sr	25	104	225	46.2	73	85	85.9	N/A	N/A	N/A	281	11.2	N/A	N/A	91	3.6
Total		75	304	705	43.1	217	252	86.1	N/A	N/A	N/A	825	11.0	N/A	N/A	223	3.0

Figure 6.2

KEVIN GREVEY

Kevin Grevey played in the NBA for 10 years with the Washington Bullets and for 2 years with the Milwaukee Bucks. I played against Kevin in the 1975 Final Four, where his Kentucky Wildcats got the best of our Syracuse Orangemen, 95-79. Kevin was the key to the Kentucky team his senior year and we had a tough time matching up with the Wildcats in that game. He had 14 points and was 4-5 from the foul line.

He shared his thoughts with me as he approached the free throw line: "I would relax my body and shoot a soft shot. My mental relaxation would visualize the ball going through the basket."

As for his routine, Kevin was a self-learner with a lot of basketball knowledge. That being said, "I would take two dribbles and then release the ball to the middle of the basket. I stressed confidence and positive vibes and could see the ball go through the basket." Part of his practice drill consisted of shooting one or two shots (i.e., one shot, two shots, etc.), always doing something else in between.

As Kevin's percentage improved from 77.8% at Kentucky to 81.7% in the NBA, he had this to offer: "I was more of a student of the game. I wanted to be better as I played with the best. We talked about techniques, understanding what you are doing, and continuing to improve. I always thought I should make them all."

Kevin is currently a scout with the Los Angeles Lakers and does broadcast work for NCAA games. He is also owner of Grevey's Restaurant and Sports Bar in Falls Church, Virginia. Grevey's has adopted the Buffalo Bills as their football team and it is considered a home away from home for all Bills fans. [See Figure 6.3][3]

Kevin Grevey
6'5", 210 lbs
Taft HS (Hamilton, OH)
University of Kentucky

Year	Class	G	FG	FGA	FG%	FT	FTA	FT%	3P	3PA	3P%	PTS	PPG	ASST	APG	REB	RPG
at the University of Kentucky																	
1972-73	So	28	236	441	53.5	52	76	68.4	N/A	N/A	N/A	524	18.7	N/A	N/A	168	6.0
1973-74	Jr	25	232	457	50.8	83	100	83.0	N/A	N/A	N/A	547	21.9	N/A	N/A	180	7.2
1974-75	Sr	31	303	592	51.2	124	157	79.0	N/A	N/A	N/A	730	23.5	N/A	N/A	199	6.4
Total		84	771	1,490	51.7	259	333	77.8	N/A	N/A	N/A	1,801	21.4	N/A	N/A	547	6.5
in the NBA																	
1975-85	N/A	672	2,915	6,670	43.7	1,389	1,701	81.7	145	434	33.4	7,364	11.0	1,247	1.9	1,594	2.4

Figure 6.3

JOHN HAVLICEK

Growing up, John Havlicek of the Boston Celtics was my favorite player. He played in the NBA for 16 years, was inducted into the NBA Hall of Fame in 1984[4], and was voted one of the 50 Greatest Players in NBA History.[5]

I realized at a young age that John Havlicek played the game of basketball the way it is supposed to be played. I wanted to try and play the same way. I can still remember listening to the transistor radio in 1965 (I was supposed to be sleeping) when John Havlicek stole the inbounds pass against the Philadelphia 76er's in game 7 of the Eastern Division Finals to preserve the victory for the Celtics. I was only 12 years old, but trying to emulate John Havlicek helped me play at Syracuse and gave me a chance at an NBA career.

When John approached the foul line, his thought process was as follows: "I put my right foot by the dot in the middle of the foul lane and my left foot at a 45-degree angle. I would concentrate on the ball going over the front of the rim, and focus."

John's foul shooting improved from 73.0% at Ohio State to 81.9% in the NBA. "Free throws are a critical part of the game. There were a lot more games in the NBA. This was a job. We were making a living making free throws." During practice, "We would shoot against each other for lunch. None of us wanted to buy lunch for any of our teammates, as we made a competition of it." [See Figure 6.4][6]

John "Hondo" Havlicek
6'5", 203 lbs
Bridgeport HS (Bridgeport, OH)
Ohio State University

at Ohio State University

Year	Class	G	FG	FGA	FG%	FT	FTA	FT%	3P	3PA	3P%	PTS	PPG	ASST	APG	REB	RPG
1959-60	So	28	144	312	46.2	53	74	71.6	N/A	N/A	N/A	341	12.2	N/A	N/A	205	7.3
1960-61	Jr	28	173	321	53.9	61	87	70.1	N/A	N/A	N/A	407	14.5	N/A	N/A	244	8.7
1961-62	Sr	28	196	377	52.0	83	109	76.1	N/A	N/A	N/A	475	17.0	N/A	N/A	271	9.7
Total		84	513	1,010	50.8	197	270	73.0	N/A	N/A	N/A	1,223	14.6	N/A	N/A	720	8.6

in the NBA

Year	Class	G	FG	FGA	FG%	FT	FTA	FT%	3P	3PA	3P%	PTS	PPG	ASST	APG	REB	RPG
1962-78	N/A	1,270	10,513	23,930	43.9	5,369	6,589	81.5	N/A	N/A	N/A	26,395	20.8	6,114	4.8	8,007	6.3

Figure 6.4

MARTY HEADD

I met Marty Headd at a basketball camp when he was in high school. I marveled at watching the kid shoot the basketball. From that moment, I knew he was going to be a very good player. Marty became a three-year starter at guard for Syracuse University and remains one of the best shooters in the school's history. He was drafted by the New York Knicks in 1981.

Marty's thought process as he approached the foul line: "Basically, it was to remain consistent and on balance and do the same thing every time."

He also offered the following comment, "The good thing about shooting – you don't need anyone else but yourself to practice and get better."

Marty lives in the Syracuse area and is employed by Syracuse University. [See Figure 6.5][7]

Marty Headd

6'2", 180 lbs

Christian Brothers Academy (Syracuse, NY)

Syracuse University

at Syracuse University

Year	Class	G	FG	FGA	FG%	FT	FTA	FT%	3P	3PA	3P%	PTS	PPG	ASST	APG	REB	RPG
1977-78	Fr	20	54	112	48.2	9	14	64.3	N/A	N/A	N/A	117	5.9	18	0.9	20	1.0
1978-79	So	30	159	302	52.6	55	67	82.1	N/A	N/A	N/A	373	12.4	47	1.6	43	1.4
1979-80	Jr	30	155	275	56.4	50	64	78.1	N/A	N/A	N/A	360	12.0	71	2.4	38	1.3
1980-81	Sr	26	130	237	54.9	49	56	87.5	N/A	N/A	N/A	309	11.9	48	1.9	50	1.9
Total		106	498	926	53.8	163	201	81.1	N/A	N/A	N/A	1,159	10.9	184	1.7	151	1.4

Figure 6.5

JEFF HORNACEK

Jeff Hornacek played 14 years in the NBA with the Phoenix Suns, Philadelphia 76er's and Utah Jazz. He has a career 87.7% free throw percentage, which is one of the best in NBA history.

Halfway through his NBA career, Jeff started to use visualization in his routine at the foul line. He told me he got the idea while listening to some business tapes. "I would line up in the center of the rim. I would visualize my whole routine. I wiped my face three times; took three dribbles; took the shot while looking at the rim; and watched it go through the basket. After this visualization, I would take the shot." His routine was his thought process when he went to the foul line.

Wiping his face three times was Jeff's way of waving to his three kids (two sons and a daughter) when they were younger; this part of his routine stuck with him throughout his NBA career.

Jeff attributes his extensive practice time and number of shots taken for his improvement from 79.0% at Iowa State to 87.7% in the NBA.

After working part-time for the Utah Jazz for the past four years, Jeff is beginning his first year as a full time assistant coach for the team. [See Figure 6.6][8]

Jeff Hornacek
6'3", 190 lbs
Lyons Township (LaGrange, IL)
Iowa State University

Year	Class	G	FG	FGA	FG%	FT	FTA	FT%	3P	3PA	3P%	PTS	PPG	ASST	APG	REB	RPG
at Iowa State University																	
1982-83	Fr	27	57	135	42.2	32	45	71.1	N/A	N/A	N/A	146	5.4	82	3.0	62	2.3
1983-84	So	29	104	208	50.0	83	105	79.0	N/A	N/A	N/A	291	10.0	198	6.8	101	3.5
1984-85	Jr	34	172	330	52.1	81	96	84.4	N/A	N/A	N/A	425	12.5	166	4.9	122	3.6
1985-86	Sr	33	177	370	47.8	97	125	77.6	N/A	N/A	N/A	451	13.7	219	6.6	127	3.8
Total		123	510	1,043	48.9	293	371	79.0	N/A	N/A	N/A	1,313	10.7	665	5.4	412	3.3
in the NBA																	
1986-2000		1,077	5,929	11,957	49.6	2,973	3,390	87.7	828	2,055	40.3	15,659	14.5	5,281	4.9	3,646	3.4

Figure 6.6

GREG "KID" KOHLS

Greg Kohls was a senior when I entered my freshman year at Syracuse. Combining his junior and senior years, he averaged over 24 points per game – which is one of the best in Syracuse's history. Greg accomplished this without the luxury of a 3-point shot. Greg is still considered one of the best shooters to play at Syracuse. His jump shot was more comparable to the NBA 3-point line than it was from the college 3-point line. Who knows how many more points Greg would have finished his career with if the 3-point shot was in existence in the early seventies. Greg was drafted by the NBA's Buffalo Braves in 1972.

Greg said he was a good free throw shooter in high school but wanted to get better. He attended Dave Bing's basketball camp where he would shoot 100 foul shots before lunch and 100 foul shots before dinner. Once he got to college, he was dedicated to excelling at free throw shooting.

As Greg approached the line, his process was as follows: "I would dribble the ball three times and concentrate on the ball going right over the front of the rim." He also added, "I would let my routine take over, which I had done so many thousands and thousands of times before. This included the same release and motion each time."

Greg is currently a resort real estate broker in northwest Florida (Sandestin). [See Figure 6.7][9]

Greg "Kid" Kohls

6'1", 170 lbs

Franklin D. Roosevelt HS (Hyde Park, NY)

Syracuse University

Year	Class	G	FG	FGA	FG%	FT	FTA	FT%	3P	3PA	3P%	PTS	PPG	ASST	APG	REB	RPG
at Syracuse University																	
1969-70	So	17	12	27	44.4	14	18	77.8	N/A	N/A	N/A	38	2.2	N/A	N/A	9	0.5
1970-71	Jr	26	211	458	46.0	152	196	77.6	N/A	N/A	N/A	574	22.1	99	3.8	87	3.3
1971-72	Sr	28	263	610	43.1	222	257	86.4	N/A	N/A	N/A	748	26.7	108	3.9	94	3.4
Total		71	486	1,095	44.4	388	471	82.4	N/A	N/A	N/A	1,360	19.2	207	2.9	190	2.7

Figure 6.7

I know at the beginning of the chapter I said the pre-requisite was that you had to have an 80% free throw percentage or better, but there is always an exception to the rule. I have to include my brother, Mike, whose percentage was 78.7% while at Syracuse. He held the consecutive free throw record of 34 made, since his junior year (1971-72). Mike held this record for 39 years, as it was just recently broken during the 2010-11 basketball season by Brandon Triche.

Mike may have been one of the best 6'3" forwards to ever play college basketball. He had a try-out with Buffalo Braves of the NBA and the Denver Nuggets of the ABA in 1973. The fact that he started for three years at forward at Syracuse probably hindered his chances at making the NBA where he had to try out at the guard position. Not only did Mike excel at basketball, he had the opportunity to sign with the Philadelphia Phillies out of high school to play baseball.

Asked his response as he approached the foul line, Mike replied, "I always tried to get fouled. I had a lot of confidence at the foul line and I knew I could make foul shots. I would let my routine take over. I concentrated on getting the ball over the front of the rim and following through."

Mike has been involved in youth basketball programs in Fayetteville, New York for the last 20 years. He owns and operates Fundamental Basketball Camp in Central New York and coaches the freshman basketball team at Fayetteville-Manlius High School. [See Figure 6.8][10]

Mike Lee
63", 190 lbs
Windsor HS (Windsor, NY)
Syracuse University

at Syracuse University

Year	Class	G	FG	FGA	FG%	FT	FTA	FT%	3P	3PA	3P%	PTS	PPG	ASST	APG	REB	RPG
1970-71	So	26	124	234	53.0	105	135	77.8	N/A	N/A	N/A	353	13.6	51	2.0	210	8.1
1971-72	Jr	28	181	326	55.5	142	171	83.0	N/A	N/A	N/A	504	18.0	61	2.2	216	7.7
1972-73	Sr	29	189	366	51.6	116	155	74.8	N/A	N/A	N/A	494	17.0	91	3.1	173	6.0
Total		83	494	926	53.3	363	461	78.7	N/A	N/A	N/A	1,351	16.3	203	2.4	599	7.2

Figure 6.8

GERRY MCNAMARA

In 2003, Gerry McNamara broke my single season free throw percentage record, which I had previously held for 30 years. This was one of my favorite records of all time. Gerry started at guard for four years at Syracuse. Today, not only does Gerry hold the single season free throw record, but he is also the career free throw percentage leader at Syracuse. After graduation, Gerry had a tryout with the Utah Jazz.

As he approached the foul line, Gerry stated, "The most important part was believing that the shot would go in. I had a lot of confidence – here's two points, and let my routine take over."

Gerry's routine was simple: "I would put my right toe at the dot, so as to be square to the basket. I would take three dribbles, spin the ball, bend my knees and finish the shot."

Gerry has been a graduate assistant at Syracuse since the 2009-10 season and is pursuing a coaching career. [See Figure 6.9][11]

Gerry McNamara
6'2", 182 lbs
Bishop Hannan HS (Scranton, PA)
Syracuse University

at Syracuse University

Year	Class	G	FG	FGA	FG%	FT	FTA	FT%	3P	3PA	3P%	PTS	PPG	ASST	APG	REB	RPG
2002-03	Fr	35	146	364	40.1	90	99	90.9	85	238	35.7	467	13.3	155	4.4	80	2.3
2003-04	So	31	153	398	38.4	123	141	87.2	105	270	28.9	534	17.2	118	3.8	80	2.6
2004-05	Jr	34	160	433	37.0	111	127	87.4	107	315	34.0	538	15.8	168	4.9	79	2.3
2005-06	Sr	35	174	490	37.0	111	123	90.2	103	308	33.4	590	16.0	207	5.9	94	2.7
Total		135	632	1,685	37.5	435	490	88.8	400	1,131	35.4	2,099	15.5	648	4.8	333	2.5

Figure 6.9

PATRICK SATALIN

I've known Patrick Satalin since his high school days and his father, Jim Satalin (National Director, Coaches vs. Cancer), is a good friend of mine. Patrick played at Catholic University where he was a starter three out of four years. His teams went to the Division III NCAA Tournament three years. Notably, during his senior year at Catholic, he made 91.2% of his foul shots.

Patrick's routine included: dribbling three times (once with his left hand, then twice with his right); placing his right foot on the nail in the middle of the foul line; locking in on the rim and letting his eyes focus; looking at the whole rim; releasing the ball; and holding his release.

When I asked Patrick what his thought process was as he approached the line, he replied, "I used the same routine and had so much confidence, I knew it was automatic. I thought here's two points, let's get back on D." At the end of games, he gave himself a friendly reminder to "stay on the line"; this was his way of reminding himself to keep his body on balance.

Patrick graduated in June 2011 with a master's degree in Public Administration from The Maxwell School at Syracuse University. [See Figure 6.10][12]

Patrick Satalin
5'11", 165 lbs
Westhill HS (Syracuse, NY)
Catholic University

at Catholic University

Year	Class	G	FG	FGA	FG%	FT	FTA	FT%	3P	3PA	3P%	PTS	PPG	ASST	APG	REB	RPG
2002-03	Fr	29	20	54	37.0	20	30	66.7	8	30	26.7	68	2.3	28	1.0	28	1.0
2003-04	So	30	103	275	37.5	75	92	81.5	61	174	35.1	342	11.4	79	2.6	73	2.4
2004-05	Jr	29	107	300	35.7	95	112	84.8	64	184	34.8	373	12.9	73	2.5	77	2.7
2005-06	Sr	28	88	257	34.2	103	113	91.2	54	166	32.5	333	11.9	84	3.0	80	2.9
Total		116	318	886	35.9	293	347	84.4	187	554	33.8	1,116	9.6	264	2.3	258	2.2

Figure 6.10

DANNY SCHAYES

Danny Schayes played at Syracuse and also had an 18-year NBA career with 8 different teams (Utah Jazz, Denver Nuggets, Milwaukee Bucks, Los Angeles Lakers, Phoenix Suns, Miami Heat, Orlando Magic, and Minnesota Timberwolves).

At 6'11", Danny's percentage was 80.6% for both his college and NBA careers. "I had a strict routine and I knew exactly what I was going to do." His routine was to relax, take three dribbles and then take a single breath in and out. "The focus from this routine, no matter what the situation, made me immune to crowd antics."

Danny offered his practice tips for shooting free throws: "I would focus on two foul shots; run; shoot two more; run; and shoot two more. I tried to emulate game conditions in my practice routine."

For the last five years, Danny has been on the board for retired NBA players. He has been working with these players in life transitions, from the basketball court to the working world. [See Figure 6.11][13]

Danny Schayes

6'11", 235 lbs
Jamesville-Dewitt HS (Dewitt, NY)
Syracuse University

Year	Class	G	FG	FGA	FG%	FT	FTA	FT%	3P	3PA	3P%	PTS	PPG	ASST	APG	REB	RPG
at Syracuse University																	
1977-78	Fr	24	39	69	56.5	34	45	75.6	N/A	N/A	N/A	112	4.7	11	0.5	96	4.0
1978-79	So	29	62	117	53.0	55	66	83.3	N/A	N/A	N/A	179	6.2	15	0.5	121	4.2
1979-80	Jr	30	59	116	50.9	60	78	76.9	N/A	N/A	N/A	178	5.9	22	0.7	134	4.5
1980-81	Sr	34	165	285	57.9	166	202	82.2	N/A	N/A	N/A	496	14.6	64	1.9	284	8.4
Total		117	325	587	55.4	315	391	80.6	N/A	N/A	N/A	965	8.2	112	1.0	635	5.4
in the NBA																	
1981-99	N/A	1,138	2,994	6,228	48.1	2,788	3,461	80.6	4	30	13.3	8,780	7.7	1,299	1.1	5,671	5.0

Figure 6.11

DOLPH SCHAYES

Dolph Schayes was inducted into the NBA Hall of Fame in 1973[14] and was voted one of the 50 Greatest Players in NBA History.[15] He played for the Syracuse Nationals for most of his NBA career and Syracuse, New York, is still his home.

"I'd always do the same thing: be relaxed with one foot in front of the other. I practiced so many foul shots. I had a lot of confidence because of my routine. Shoot over the front of the rim and follow through."

After a few years in the NBA, Dolph put a 14-inch rim inside the basketball rim in order to improve his foul shooting during practice sessions. "I used to put the smaller rim inside the rim. It made me over-exaggerate my arc on the foul shot. I worked very hard on my arc. Then when the 14-inch rim was removed, the basket appeared much bigger to me."

Dolph offered this thought for smaller or younger kids that aren't quite strong enough for a 15-foot foul shot: "Smaller kids should start out shooting free throws from 10 feet instead of 15 feet so they can use the proper form."

Dolph averaged 10.2 ppg at NYU from 1944-48. No other information was available from his college playing days. [See Figure 6.12][16]

Dolph Schayes

6'7", 195 lbs
Dewitt Clinton HS (Bronx, NY)
New York University

Year	Class	G	FG	FGA	FG%	FT	FTA	FT%	3P	3PA	3P%	PTS	PPG	ASST	APG	REB	RPG
in the NBA																	
1949-64	N/A	996	5,863	15,447	38.0	**6,712**	**7,904**	**84.9**	N/A	N/A	N/A	18,438	18.5	3,072	3.1	11,256	12.1

Figure 6.12

JOHN STOCKTON

John Stockton played 19 years with the Utah Jazz. He was voted one of the 50 Greatest Players in NBA History[17] and was inducted into the NBA Hall of Fame in 2009.[18] One thing that I admired most about John Stockton was his loyalty to the Utah Jazz. You don't see it often in this day and age – a professional player playing his whole career with the same team.

John's thought process varied over his NBA career as he was always his own coach when it came to foul shooting. "In general, I approached the foul line with a sense of balance. I would relax my shoulders so the mechanics of the shot could take over. I let all the practice and muscle memory take over, like a walk in the park."

John improved his free throw percentage to 82.6% in the NBA compared to 71.9% at Gonzaga. I asked John what he attributed the improvement to. "It's a matter of mathematics. In the NBA, everything is a two-shot foul. There are no one and one's as in the college game. It takes a little pressure off. There is a lot more shooting in the NBA."

John resides in Spokane, Washington, where he grew up, and enjoys coaching. He has six children. [See Figure 6.13][19]

John Stockton

6'1", 170 lbs

Gonzaga Prep (Spokane, WA)

Gonzaga University

Year	Class	G	FG	FGA	FG%	FT	FTA	FT%	3P	3PA	3P%	PTS	PPG	ASST	APG	REB	RPG
at Gonzaga University																	
1980-81	Fr	25	26	45	57.8	26	35	74.3	N/A	N/A	N/A	78	3.1	34	1.4	11	0.4
1981-82	So	27	117	203	57.6	69	102	67.6	N/A	N/A	N/A	303	11.2	135	5.0	67	2.5
1982-83	Jr	27	142	274	51.8	91	115	79.1	N/A	N/A	N/A	375	13.9	184	6.8	87	3.2
1983-84	Sr	28	229	397	57.7	126	182	69.2	N/A	N/A	N/A	584	20.9	201	7.2	66	2.4
Total		107	514	919	55.9	312	434	71.9	N/A	N/A	N/A	1,340	12.5	554	5.2	231	2.2
in the NBA																	
1984-2003	N/A	1,504	7,039	13,658	51.5	4,788	5,796	82.6	845	2,203	38.4	19,711	13.1	15,806	10.5	4,051	2.7

Figure 6.13

As you read the previous comments, pay special attention to the similarities as each player approached the foul line. From my point of view, I believe that anyone who has a career free throw percentage of 80% or above (high school, college, and/or the NBA) should consider themselves in the upper echelon of the best free throw shooters in the world.

For those of us who never made it to the highest level, odds are that our percentages would have kept improving if we continued to play. This is evidenced by the statistics of the NBA players, who show improvement throughout their careers. The free throw percentage improvement from college to the NBA was as follows: Junior Bridgeman, +7.6%; Kevin Grevey, +3.9%; John Havlicek, +8.9%; Jeff Hornacek, +8.7%, and John Stockton, +10.7%. **This just goes to show you that there is no age limit that can keep you from improving.**

How many times did you see practice, repetition, or routine get mentioned? Notice how the players spoke about balance, being relaxed, and squaring to the basket. The players talked about being positive, blocking out everything, concentration, confidence, focus, and visualization. Being consistent, the same mindset, the same motion, the follow through and the release are also mentioned by the majority of the players.

Whether you are an NBA player or fall a bit short of the professional level, all good free throw shooters have a lot in common – **all have a routine they fall back on when approaching the foul line.**

Going forward in your basketball career – from the driveway to the NBA – have a routine, practice, have the proper mindset, and set goals. The best foul shooters in the game have a routine. If you want to be one of the best, the place to start is the beginning – develop a routine or a process.

7

BENCHMARK

Establish your goal by practicing *every day*.

MONTHLY BENCHMARK – JANUARY			
Date	**Free Throws Made (FTM)**	**Free Throws Attempted (FTA)**	**Free Throw Percentage %**
1-Jan			
2-Jan			
3-Jan			
4-Jan			
5-Jan			
6-Jan			
7-Jan			
8-Jan			
9-Jan			
10-Jan			
11-Jan			
12-Jan			
13-Jan			
14-Jan			
15-Jan			
16-Jan			
17-Jan			
18-Jan			
19-Jan			
20-Jan			
21-Jan			
22-Jan			
23-Jan			
24-Jan			
25-Jan			
26-Jan			
27-Jan			
28-Jan			
29-Jan			
30-Jan			
31-Jan			
Total			

	MONTHLY BENCHMARK – FEBRUARY		
Date	**Free Throws Made (FTM)**	**Free Throws Attempted (FTA)**	**Free Throw Percentage %**
1-Feb			
2-Feb			
3-Feb			
4-Feb			
5-Feb			
6-Feb			
7-Feb			
8-Feb			
9-Feb			
10-Feb			
11-Feb			
12-Feb			
13-Feb			
14-Feb			
15-Feb			
16-Feb			
17-Feb			
18-Feb			
19-Feb			
20-Feb			
21-Feb			
22-Feb			
23-Feb			
24-Feb			
25-Feb			
26-Feb			
27-Feb			
28-Feb			
29-Feb			
Total			

MONTHLY BENCHMARK – MARCH			
Date	**Free Throws Made (FTM)**	**Free Throws Attempted (FTA)**	**Free Throw Percentage %**
1-Mar			
2-Mar			
3-Mar			
4-Mar			
5-Mar			
6-Mar			
7-Mar			
8-Mar			
9-Mar			
10-Mar			
11-Mar			
12-Mar			
13-Mar			
14-Mar			
15-Mar			
16-Mar			
17-Mar			
18-Mar			
19-Mar			
20-Mar			
21-Mar			
22-Mar			
23-Mar			
24-Mar			
25-Mar			
26-Mar			
27-Mar			
28-Mar			
29-Mar			
30-Mar			
31-Mar			
Total			

MONTHLY BENCHMARK – APRIL			
Date	**Free Throws Made (FTM)**	**Free Throws Attempted (FTA)**	**Free Throw Percentage %**
1-Apr			
2-Apr			
3-Apr			
4-Apr			
5-Apr			
6-Apr			
7-Apr			
8-Apr			
9-Apr			
10-Apr			
11-Apr			
12-Apr			
13-Apr			
14-Apr			
15-Apr			
16-Apr			
17-Apr			
18-Apr			
19-Apr			
20-Apr			
21-Apr			
22-Apr			
23-Apr			
24-Apr			
25-Apr			
26-Apr			
27-Apr			
28-Apr			
29-Apr			
30-Apr			
Total			

MONTHLY BENCHMARK – MAY			
Date	**Free Throws Made (FTM)**	**Free Throws Attempted (FTA)**	**Free Throw Percentage %**
1-May			
2-May			
3-May			
4-May			
5-May			
6-May			
7-May			
8-May			
9-May			
10-May			
11-May			
12-May			
13-May			
14-May			
15-May			
16-May			
17-May			
18-May			
19-May			
20-May			
21-May			
22-May			
23-May			
24-May			
25-May			
26-May			
27-May			
28-May			
29-May			
30-May			
31-May			
Total			

Date	Free Throws Made (FTM)	Free Throws Attempted (FTA)	Free Throw Percentage %
MONTHLY BENCHMARK – JUNE			
1-Jun			
2-Jun			
3-Jun			
4-Jun			
5-Jun			
6-Jun			
7-Jun			
8-Jun			
9-Jun			
10-Jun			
11-Jun			
12-Jun			
13-Jun			
14-Jun			
15-Jun			
16-Jun			
17-Jun			
18-Jun			
19-Jun			
20-Jun			
21-Jun			
22-Jun			
23-Jun			
24-Jun			
25-Jun			
26-Jun			
27-Jun			
28-Jun			
29-Jun			
30-Jun			
Total			

MONTHLY BENCHMARK – JULY			
Date	Free Throws Made (FTM)	Free Throws Attempted (FTA)	Free Throw Percentage %
1-Jul			
2-Jul			
3-Jul			
4-Jul			
5-Jul			
6-Jul			
7-Jul			
8-Jul			
9-Jul			
10-Jul			
11-Jul			
12-Jul			
13-Jul			
14-Jul			
15-Jul			
16-Jul			
17-Jul			
18-Jul			
19-Jul			
20-Jul			
21-Jul			
22-Jul			
23-Jul			
24-Jul			
25-Jul			
26-Jul			
27-Jul			
28-Jul			
29-Jul			
30-Jul			
31-Jul			
Total			

MONTHLY BENCHMARK – AUGUST			
Date	**Free Throws Made (FTM)**	**Free Throws Attempted (FTA)**	**Free Throw Percentage %**
1-Aug			
2-Aug			
3-Aug			
4-Aug			
5-Aug			
6-Aug			
7-Aug			
8-Aug			
9-Aug			
10-Aug			
11-Aug			
12-Aug			
13-Aug			
14-Aug			
15-Aug			
16-Aug			
17-Aug			
18-Aug			
19-Aug			
20-Aug			
21-Aug			
22-Aug			
23-Aug			
24-Aug			
25-Aug			
26-Aug			
27-Aug			
28-Aug			
29-Aug			
30-Aug			
31-Aug			
Total			

MONTHLY BENCHMARK – SEPTEMBER			
Date	**Free Throws Made (FTM)**	**Free Throws Attempted (FTA)**	**Free Throw Percentage %**
1-Sep			
2-Sep			
3-Sep			
4-Sep			
5-Sep			
6-Sep			
7-Sep			
8-Sep			
9-Sep			
10-Sep			
11-Sep			
12-Sep			
13-Sep			
14-Sep			
15-Sep			
16-Sep			
17-Sep			
18-Sep			
19-Sep			
20-Sep			
21-Sep			
22-Sep			
23-Sep			
24-Sep			
25-Sep			
26-Sep			
27-Sep			
28-Sep			
29-Sep			
30-Sep			
Total			

MONTHLY BENCHMARK – OCTOBER

Date	Free Throws Made (FTM)	Free Throws Attempted (FTA)	Free Throw Percentage %
1-Oct			
2-Oct			
3-Oct			
4-Oct			
5-Oct			
6-Oct			
7-Oct			
8-Oct			
9-Oct			
10-Oct			
11-Oct			
12-Oct			
13-Oct			
14-Oct			
15-Oct			
16-Oct			
17-Oct			
18-Oct			
19-Oct			
20-Oct			
21-Oct			
22-Oct			
23-Oct			
24-Oct			
25-Oct			
26-Oct			
27-Oct			
28-Oct			
29-Oct			
30-Oct			
31-Oct			
Total			

MONTHLY BENCHMARK – NOVEMBER			
Date	**Free Throws Made (FTM)**	**Free Throws Attempted (FTA)**	**Free Throw Percentage %**
1-Nov			
2-Nov			
3-Nov			
4-Nov			
5-Nov			
6-Nov			
7-Nov			
8-Nov			
9-Nov			
10-Nov			
11-Nov			
12-Nov			
13-Nov			
14-Nov			
15-Nov			
16-Nov			
17-Nov			
18-Nov			
19-Nov			
20-Nov			
21-Nov			
22-Nov			
23-Nov			
24-Nov			
25-Nov			
26-Nov			
27-Nov			
28-Nov			
29-Nov			
30-Nov			
Total			

MONTHLY BENCHMARK – DECEMBER			
Date	**Free Throws Made (FTM)**	**Free Throws Attempted (FTA)**	**Free Throw Percentage %**
1-Dec			
2-Dec			
3-Dec			
4-Dec			
5-Dec			
6-Dec			
7-Dec			
8-Dec			
9-Dec			
10-Dec			
11-Dec			
12-Dec			
13-Dec			
14-Dec			
15-Dec			
16-Dec			
17-Dec			
18-Dec			
19-Dec			
20-Dec			
21-Dec			
22-Dec			
23-Dec			
24-Dec			
25-Dec			
26-Dec			
27-Dec			
28-Dec			
29-Dec			
30-Dec			
31-Dec			
Total			

AFTERWORD

FOUL SHOOTING AND ENTREPRENEURSHIP
By Ted Lachowicz
President – EBV Foundation

Syracuse University founded the Entrepreneurship Bootcamp for Veterans with Disabilities (EBV) program in 2007. EBV offers cutting edge, experiential training in entrepreneurship and small business management to our Armed Forces disabled as a result of their service supporting operations Enduring Freedom and Iraqi Freedom http://whitman.syr.edu/ebv/. Since its inception the program is now offered at 8 world-class business schools and over 300 disabled veterans have graduated from EBV. In 2008, as an effort to lend my support to Syracuse University, I founded the EBV Foundation www.ebvfoundation.org

Jim became aware of the great efforts by our alma mater and not only donates a portion of the proceeds from the Harold Lee Open Golf Tournament he hosts each year, but has also graciously agreed to donate fifty percent of proceeds from the sales of this book to the Syracuse EBV program. This book will not only help readers excel in foul shooting, but will allow many disabled veterans to obtain the opportunity to live their dream and start a small business with the help of the EBV program. It is hard to argue the world is not a better place because of Jim Lee's big heart.

Every year, I speak to the Syracuse University EBV class and discuss my experience as an entrepreneur to help the students understand the complexities of starting a small business. Over the past several years, I have mentored many of the EBV graduates as they start their new life as an entrepreneur. So when Jim invited me to write a chapter comparing foul shooting to entrepreneurship I initially thought it was not possible. After reading a draft of *Fifteen Feet For Free*, I was able to draw strong comparisons between the two and realized the qualities of a successful entrepreneur are similar to the qualities of a successful foul shooter.

The six requirements that not only make a successful entrepreneur, but also a successful foul shooter are as follows:

1. Set Goals. Although goals for foul shooters are covered in Section 5 of this book, I want to touch upon the importance of it again. Over 30 years ago, while I was working at Ryder Truck Rental, a consultant came to speak to the sales force about setting realistic goals. What the consultant said had an extreme impact on how I start any business project and to this day I share it with every entrepreneur that crosses my path.

The consultant asked what the best word to describe a goal is:

1. Is it something you would like to achieve?
2. Is it a target?
3. Is it mandatory?
4. Is it a guideline?

Only seven percent of the people in the seminar got the right answer. The most common answer was a guideline or a target. However, the correct answer is **mandatory**.

To put this into perspective the example given was, next time you are on an airplane, go to the pilot and ask if his goal is to get you to your destination safely. If his definition of a goal is anything other than mandatory, get off the plane. It has to be mandatory to achieve his goal and get you there safely.

Setting a goal as an entrepreneur or as a foul shooter is the same. The goal must be mandatory to achieve, no excuses.

It is, however, important to set realistic goals, but that goal must be mandatory. That is why I suggested an eighty-five percent foul shooting percentage. It is a realistic goal that can and must be achieved.

2. Make a Game/Business Plan. Every successful business must have a business plan. A failed entrepreneur with no business plan or a very poor business plan is an entrepreneur that never tried. Business plans allow entrepreneurs to define a path to success. A foul shooter needs a game plan to achieve their goals. Consider this book *Fifteen*

Feet For Free as your game plan. It provides you with step-by-step instructions how to significantly improve your foul shooting skills. Read it, study it, reread it and most importantly implement it.

3. Take Initiative. To start a successful business you must take the initiative, make decisions and have unwavering discipline. The best athletes don't need to be told to practice, practice, and practice some more. They know what they have to do to be the best and by taking initiative they have an advantage over their competitors. Short cuts are not an option to success in business or sports. No one can or should make you take that initiative, whether your parents, teammates, or coach. Your success is up to you. I tell the EBV students, you will get as much success in your small business as the amount of effort you put in. Same rule applies to basketball; you will become a great foul shooter based on the sweat and struggle you put in.

4. Motivation, Drive, Determination and Passion. As an entrepreneur you have to have the motivation, drive, determination and passion to be successful. You cannot and will not succeed unless you truly want to be the best you can be. In foul shooting, being the first one on the court and the last one to leave is the passion that makes the best athletes who they are today. No matter how many times you fail allow your inner motivation to pick you back up and try again. Success comes from believing in you and out working everyone else.

I have mentored over thirty EBV disabled veterans and in every case, the successful entrepreneurs are the determined ones. When an EBV student looks at me and says they are determined at all costs to start their business and be successful, I recognize a winner. The young basketball player who is determined to become the best foul shooter and that determination drives their practice time and effort will see results in the game.

5. Focus. You have your goal, your game plan, and you are determined to succeed; now it is up to you to execute. Failure to focus is the catalyst to many unsuccessful entrepreneurs. As a foul shooter, you need to focus on every little detail this book has to offer. Jim averaged over 85% in free throw shooting during his career at Syracuse University. He was successful because he focused on the details.

Practice is important and critical to success, but if you are practicing wrong you will not get the results you desire. Don't be afraid to reread every chapter and memorize every detail. Stay focused and you will see positive results.

6. Get Excited about the End Game. The new entrepreneur must be excited on achieving results. They are successful because this desire to achieve results motivates them to out work their competitors. Today some of the best players in professional sports and most successful entrepreneurs are the over-achievers.

Many players have an incredible talent, but not all athletes, like entrepreneurs, are created equal. It is up to you to utilize the tools given to you to become the best foul shooter on the team, in fact the league. Entrepreneurs and athletes alike must recognize and implement the six points listed above to avoid falling short of their dream of success.

I want to thank Jim for all he has done for the EBV program at Syracuse and the disabled veteran community. I met Jim Lee over 35 years ago at Syracuse University and I am honored today to call him a friend.

EPILOGUE

Hopefully, *Fifteen Feet For Free* offers another avenue to help our disabled veterans.

As of the writing of this book, the annual Harold Lee Open Golf Tournament has helped to purchase six vans for the Disabled American Veterans (DAV) Transportation Department for New York State; assisted in renovating a family consultation room at the Veterans Administrations (VA) Medical Center in Syracuse, New York; leased a bus for Syracuse's VA Medical Center which can carry four wheelchairs and eight ambulatory patients; donated $27,500 to *The Wounded Warrior Project*; and donated $42,942 to the *Entrepreneurship Bootcamp for Veterans* with Disabilities (EBV) at Syracuse University's Martin J. Whitman School of Management. Going forward, I hope to expand these contributions.

I believe we were all put on this earth to help one another and contribute to society in a meaningful way. By watching my dad live his life, I recognized some amazing attributes I hope I can live up to.

If this book helps at least one person become a better free throw shooter or helps one person overcome an injury or a disability by just changing their outlook on life, it will be a success in my eyes.

If you would like to help our veterans with disabilities by making a separate donation, please feel free to send your donation to:

The Harold Lee Fund [a 501 (c) (3) corporation]
Attention: Jim Lee
4513 Wilderness Way
Syracuse, New York 13215
Memo: EBV Program – Fifteen Feet For Free

For more information and updates on the Harold Lee Fund and the EBV Program, go to the *Fifteen Feet For Free* website, http://fifteenfeetforfree.com/.

NOTES

Chapter 2—Purpose
1. www.orangehoops.org/JLee.htm

Chapter 3—Practice
1. *Definition of practice,* http://www.merriam-webster.com/dictionary/practice

Chapter 4—Mindset
1. *Psycho-Cybernetics,* by Maxwell Maltz, M.D, F.I.C.S.; published by POCKET BOOKS, a division of Simon & Schuster, Inc., 29th printing . . . May, 1975; Copyright, 1960, by Prentice-Hall, Inc.; "Imagination Practice Can Lower your Golf Score", pg 38-39.

Chapter 6—Philosophies
1. www.basketball-reference.com/players/b/bridgju01.html
2. www.orangehoops.org/RCornwall.htm
3. www.basketball-reference.com/players/g/greveke01.html
4. www.basketball-reference.com/players/h/havlijo01.html
5. www.nba.com/history/50greatest.html
6. www.basketball-reference.com/players/h/havlijo01.html
7. www.orangehoops.org/MHeadd.htm
8. www.basketball-reference.com/players/h/hornaje01.html
9. www.orangehoops.org/GKohls.htm
10. www.orangehoops.org/MLee.htm
11. www.orangehoops.org/GMcNamara.htm
12. www.cuacardinals.com/sports/mbkb/archives/index
    2002-03, 2003-04, 2004-05, 2005-06 stats
13. www.basketball-reference.com/players/s/schayda01.html
14. www.basketball-reference.com/players/s/schaydo01.html
15. www.nba.com/history/50greatest.html

16. www.basketball-reference.com/players/s/schaydo01.html
17. www.nba.com/history/50greatest.html
18. www.basketball-reference.com/players/s/stockjo01.html
19. www.basketball-reference.com/players/s/stockjo01.html

ACKNOWLEDGEMENTS

I would like to thank my wife, Lou Ann, and my children, Amanda, Jay, and Suzanne for helping me with this project. If it wasn't for them, I wouldn't have been able to finish the book. Amanda helped me edit the book and Suzanne helped with the illustrations. A special thank you goes out to my mother for being there every day during our youth as we grew up.

For all my friends who play in the Harold Lee Open Golf Tournament each year, if it wasn't for you and the success we have had, I might not have ever taken this next step.

My thanks to Pat Donnelly for helping me get this project started and off the ground. To Mike Waters, who gave me good advice and ideas along the way. A special thank you goes to Kevin Armstrong for reviewing the book once it was completed. Ray Toenniessen was a big help providing information and input regarding the EBV program.

I am blessed to have good friends and acquaintances that agreed to be interviewed in order to enhance this project. Junior Bridgeman, Richie Cornwall, Kevin Grevey, John Havlicek, Marty Headd, Jeff Hornacek, Greg Kohls, Mike Lee, Gerry McNamara, Patrick Satalin, Danny Schayes, Dolph Schayes, and John Stockton – I say thank you for giving me the opportunity to try and help our veterans with disabilities. Many thanks go to Ted Lachowicz, who so eloquently tied together Foul Shooting and Entrepreneurship.

I am grateful to Pam Davis, Mike Gehm, Bob Korman, Frank Layden, Anthony "Anto" Martens, Joe Olin, Christopher Petosa, John Petosa, Marty Salanger, and Jim Widrick for helping me to facilitate parts of this process.

For those who had confidence in me and were willing to endorse this venture to help me out, I will never forget what you did for me – Jim Boeheim, Jack Catanzaro, Bob Costas, Pat Donnelly, Tim Giarrusso, Jack Halloran, Mike Haynie, Mike Perlis, Jim Roy, Jim Satalin, Steve Shaw, and Morgan Wootten.

If it wasn't for my brother Mike, I would never have been in a position to write this book. I played with, and against, him throughout my youth. He included me in all sports. He beat me up in each sport and never made anything easy for me. It was the best thing that ever happened to me. He made me pay attention to detail, learn the fundamentals, become a smart player, work harder, work smarter, and be the best I could possibly be. Thank you, Mike.

Lastly, I have to thank my father. You were my hero. I tried to do the best I could and I know that I am a better person because of you.

ABOUT THE AUTHOR

While at Syracuse University, Jim Lee was one of the best foul shooters in the country. Since graduating in 1975, he has been helping people of all ages with their foul shooting. His thoughts, techniques and fundamental instruction should make foul shooting simple and easy to understand for just about every player, at every level.

Jim has been in the Petroleum and Energy Industry for over 20 years and is currently the Eastern New York Market Manager with Noco Energy Corp., out of Buffalo, New York.

Jim lives in Syracuse, New York with his wife Lou Ann; they have three children, Amanda, Jay and Suzanne. He enjoys being with his family, golfing, reading and swimming.

HOOP NOTES

HOOP NOTES

HOOP NOTES